THE CASSIRER LECTURES

# HUSSERL AND THE
# SEARCH FOR CERTITUDE

Leszek Kolakowski

Yale University Press
New Haven and London 1975

Published with assistance from the
Ernst Cassirer Publication Fund

Library of Congress catalog card number: 74-29724
International standard book number: 0-300-01858-4

Designed by Sally Sullivan
and set in CRT Baskerville type.
Printed in the United States of America by
Colonial Press Inc., Clinton, Massachusetts.

Published in Great Britain, Europe, and Africa by
Yale University Press, Ltd., London.
Distributed in Latin America by Kaiman & Polon,
Inc., New York City; in India by UBS Publishers' Distributors Pvt.,
Ltd., Delhi; in Japan by John Weatherhill, Inc., Tokyo.

# CONTENTS

## NOTE

These are three lectures delivered at Yale University in February 1974. In preparing them I borrowed some fragments from my article written in German under the title "Das Suchen nach der Gewissheit" and published in a collection, *Information und Imagination*, by Piper Verlag, Munich, 1973. I borrowed, in addition, a small fragment from my book written in Polish and published in Polish and German respectively by the Institut Litteraire in Paris and by Piper Verlag in Munich (the German title is *Die Gegenwärtigkeit des Mythos*, 1972). I am very grateful to Mrs. Jane Isay for her great effort in translating this text from a bizarre idiom unknown to scholars, into English.

# FIRST LECTURE: THE ENDS

*Why I think the topic is important*  Husserl appears here rather as something of a pretext for discussing the question of certainty. This pretext, however, is far from a pretext that could be arbitrary; and it would be difficult indeed to find a better one. I do not pretend to be an expert on Husserl, as are many people, who analyze every step in his intellectual development, who seize upon even the most minute changes in his formulations, and who try to reconcile everything he said. Neither do I believe, as do some, that if one goes deeply enough into his work, one might be, as it were, initiated into a method of thinking which is absolutely reliable. Without being interested in this kind of inquiry, I do admit that Husserl was indeed a great philosopher because of the extraordinary obstinacy of his endless endeavor: to restore hope in the return to absolutely primordial insight in cognition and to achieve victory over relativism and skepticism. Reading Husserl is often irritating. During his life he piled up a great number of very detailed distinctions and concepts which can easily mislead the reader who is not devoting his life to Husserl studies. Quite often the reader gets the impression that these distinctions are being made on empty material. Quite often phenomenology appears to the reader as an eternal program that is never applied; a method being endlessly perfected, but rarely shown *in actu* (and we know that in philosophy, in contrast to technology, to describe a method is never sufficient to enable people to apply it—the method is never clear until it is demonstrated in operation).

Bergson was probably right in saying that every philosopher in his life says only one thing, one leading idea or intention that endows all his works with meaning. We can grasp such a basic intuition incessantly present in the whole, gigantic effort of Husserl. Like most philosophers, he was writing the same book throughout his life, always going back to the beginning, correcting himself, struggling with his own presuppositions. The goal was invariably the same: how to discover the unshakable, the absolutely unquestionable foundation of knowledge; how to refute arguments of skeptics, of relativists; how to fend off the corrosion of psychologism and historicism; how to reach a perfectly hard ground in cognition. I myself was strongly *negatively* dependent on Husserl. I think that he did not discover this self-supporting foundation of our thought. But not only was his effort not in vain; I believe that the phenomenology was the greatest and the most serious attempt in our century to reach the ultimate sources of knowledge. It is of the utmost importance to philosophy to ask: why did this attempt fail and why (as I think) was it bound to fail?

*The skeptical disease: freedom from science*   At first glance, phenomenology appears to be a very "technical" kind of philosophy. It strives to be a "science," not a Weltanschauung. But its impulse toward a Weltanschauung peeps out again and again. Husserl himself expected that his method would play a great role in saving European culture from skeptical decay. Like any philosopher, he is intelligible only in contrast to, and against the background of, the philosophical culture he was attacking. In many of his works, his antididactic way of writing discouraged readers: for Husserl the discipline of content was the only thing that counted. And so, his impulse toward a Weltanschauung is often concealed. Sometimes nevertheless it appears clearly (as in *Philosophie als strenge Wissenschaft* or in *Crisis*). And, after all, without knowing that we would not know what his philosophy is for.

The concept of certainty can be regarded as the key to Husserl's thought. He noticed that the project of scientific philosophy in the sense popularized by German thinkers in the second half of the nineteenth century was misleading and dangerous. The slogan of "scientificity" smuggled a renunciation of what had passed for science in the genuine—Platonic—sense throughout the European intellectual tradition. It blurred the basic distinction between *doxa* and *epistēme*, between opinion and knowledge. In giving up the tradition of German idealism, philosophy gave up its independence from the sciences. It started regarding itself either as a synthesis of the sciences or as a psychological analysis. Even new variants of Kantianism shifted to the psychological standpoint and explained the Kantian a priori not as a set of transcendental conditions of knowledge (valid for any rational being) but as specific qualities of the human psyche, and this led fatefully to generic relativism.

Husserl's concept of "scientific philosophy" was entirely different. Philosophy must not accept any ready-made results from the sciences and "generalize" them. Its calling is to inquire into the meaning and foundation of these results. Philosophy does not have to be a "crown" or a synthesis, but a meaning-founding activity which logically precedes the sciences, as they are incapable of interpreting themselves. The idea of an epistemology based on a science, on psychology in particular, is revoltingly absurd.

To believe in a psychological epistemology amounts to believing that we are allowed to accept the results of one particular science in order to legitimate the claims of any science to objectivity or to endow with meaning all sciences, and this obviously involves a vicious circle. Thus Husserl took over the antiskeptical tradition of European philosophy—the tradition of Plato, Descartes, Leibniz, and Kant, all of whom had asked (1) What may be doubted and what may not? (2) Are we entitled to ask (and to answer) not only "how is the world?" but also "how is the world bound to be?" and what is the sense and the purpose of the latter question?

Husserl believed that the search for certitude was constitutive of European culture and that giving up this search would amount to destroying that culture. Husserl was probably right: the history of science and philosophy in Europe would indeed be unintelligible if we neglected the pursuit of such a certitude, a certitude that is more than practically satisfying; a pursuit of truth as distinct from the pursuit of technically reliable knowledge. We do not have to explain why we look for certainty when doubt hinders our practical life; but the need for certainty is not so obvious when no direct, indirect, or even possible, practical considerations are involved. Every high-school student is taught that geometry, in conformity with its name, originated from the need to measure land. Still, it would be hard to explain how, in measuring the land, the axiomatic system of Euclid—the system we admire today as a miracle—was necessary. We know what arithmetic is for, but no practical needs could have incited Euclid to build his well-known beautiful proof that the set of prime numbers is infinite. One can hardly imagine how the knowledge that the set of prime numbers is infinite, rather than finite, would make any practical difference at all. No practical considerations can explain the great turning points in the history of knowledge, even if their results later prove to be of great practical use. That this is often the case proves that if people had not expected to derive from their knowledge more than technical use, and had not sought after truth and certitude as values in themselves, they would not have produced technically fruitful science. This bears out the idea that it ultimately pays in science to neglect its possible usefulness, but it does not explain why people actually did neglect it: only the fruit, not the reasons of this search are revealed to us.

The task that European philosophy assumed from the very beginning, not only from Descartes, was this: to destroy apparent certitudes in order to gain "genuine" ones; to cast doubt on everything, in order to free oneself from doubting. As a rule, its destructive results proved to be more efficient and more convincing than its positive programs; philosophers have always been stronger in shat-

tering old certitudes than in establishing new
ones. There were two realms where common sense
sought the sources of certainty: direct perceptions
and the truths of mathematics (at least those
directly intelligible). The question of certainty
appeared when philosophers started criticizing
the certainty of perception, discussing the illusions
of senses, stigmatizing eyes and ears as "bad
witnesses," and attributing sensible qualities to
the perceiver, rather than to what was perceived.
The distinction between "correct" perceptions
and illusions could hardly remove doubts, since it
was easy to notice that what we know about the
world we know from perceptions. Then, we have
in principle no means of confronting the content
of perceptions with the original we know from
other sources, and to check their conformity. And
it was objected, to mathematical propositions,
that their seeming certitude was grounded only in
their being empty tautologies which tell us nothing about the world. This suspicion that mathematical knowledge owed its certitude to its analytical character had already appeared among
ancient skeptics in a somewhat different form: as
the objection that deductive reasoning implies
always a *petitio principii* because the conclusions are
always included in the premises. This gave skeptics the basis for their pragmatic interpretation of
knowledge—since we can never reach the ulti-

mate sources of certitude, we should consider our
knowledge not as being true in the current sense
but as a set of practical instructions, orientation
signs, which are indispensable in escaping suffer-
ing but do not tell us how the world is, let alone
how it is bound to be. The ancient skeptics said
virtually everything that modern positivism would
say: there are no synthetic a priori judgments;
and whatever is necessary in our knowledge is
included entirely in analytical judgments that
regulate our use of language but otherwise are
empty. What is certain are the contents of singular perceptions of which the subsequent accumulation in a so-called "law of nature" is necessary
for life but logically arbitrary, for we cannot
legitimate induction without inductive reasoning,
that is without a vicious circle. Empirical knowledge does not differ from conditioned reflexes,
except that human beings, unlike other animals,
have better ways of accumulating it and handing
it over to their descendants. What we really know
are useless singular perceptions about whose ontological meaning we must not ask; if we go beyond
this knowledge it is not because we are logically
entitled to do so, but because we could not live
otherwise. Next to the analytical truths of mathematics (and logic) and empirical statements that
are imprisoned in their *hic et nunc,* there are only
some very important statements of the empirical

sciences which have great practical use, but it would be an abuse to call them "truth." Since we build ships and boats, we have to behave as if Archimedes' law were valid—otherwise we would drown. But we have no reason to maintain that there is such a lasting property of the world as Archimedes' law.

*Vain attempts at defining certitude*  Transcendental thought in its various forms rebelled against these irritating conclusions. Descartes made two distinctions whose validity is decisive for the destiny of the question of certitude:

(1) The distinction between the subjective feeling of evidence ("obviousness") and the objective evidence of truth.

(2) The distinction between "moral" and metaphysical certitude.

Both turned out to be of little help. That the feeling of evidence is not the same as the knowledge that the evidence dwells in the act of perceiving, we gather only from the fact that we are often compelled to reject, later on, this feeling as illusory (induced by a pathological state of mind), but this does not imply that we have a criterion that enables us to distinguish "subjective" certainty from "genuine" certainty which emanates from the object. And Descartes was unable to establish such a criterion without the help of divine veracity, which restored our trust in common sense. But the first critics noticed a vicious circle in his reasoning: Descartes had made use of the criterion of evidence in order to prove the existence of God, and then he used God to validate the criterion of evidence.

We are hardly better off when discussing the second distinction, between moral and metaphysical certitude. We are morally certain of a judgment (according to Descartes) if it is grounded to such a degree that we may accept it for all practical purposes and use in reasoning. Metaphysical certitude gives quality to judgments which makes them not only practically reliable but apodictically unshakable. Again, to convince ourselves that there are such judgments we have to call in divine veracity. To Descartes, the difference is not one of the degree of probability but a difference of character. For all practical purposes moral certitude is enough. For Descartes, more is required not to improve our technical skills, but to help us discover a meaningful world-order and our place in it; and this includes not only the act of cogito but the whole chain of reasoning leading to the divine Founder of Being.

If Descartes had stopped after the first step, after "cogito," his discovery would have been sterile. I would know nothing more than "I am" without being able to say what this 'am' means or to endow this truth with a universal meaning. In fact, cogito can be only expressed in the first person singular, and it would be absurd to say "John thinks, then John exists." Descartes himself emphasized that the cogito, in spite of the "ergo" it contains, was not properly an inference but one indivisible act, an act in which I grasp my own existence as that of a thinking being. It is only after the real existence of God appears as apodictically proven, and with Him—the meaningful order of the world and the trust in our senses are restored—that we know what "metaphysical certitude" is for. But this passage from cogito to God revealed, from the very beginning, so many logical lacunas that the effects of Descartes' efforts turned out to contradict his intentions: his strictures on the reliability of current ways of cognition seemed much stronger than his endeavor to build a firm foundation for a new kind of certainty; the skeptical side operated better than the logically fragile reconstruction of the universe in a meaningful order.

It is useful to go back to Descartes not because he restored old objections to the reliability of perception and thereby gave the strongest impetus to modern idealism, but because his distinction between moral and metaphysical certitude provided the opportunity to distinguish truth from probability in such a way that "probable" turned out not to be "similar to the truth," not "coming closer to the truth," not "an inexact, imperfectly grounded truth," but rather the mere appearance of truth, a pseudo-truth. It turned out that once we gave up the idea of an apodictically certain (and not analytical) truth, we did not need, and we were not capable of building, any concept of truth at all; once we are unable to say how the world is bound to be, we are unable to say how it is, either. This was the important result of later positivist criticism: when absolute truth and metaphysical certainty disappear the truth *tout court* disappears as well; once we reject synthetic a priori judgments, the concept of truth is empty. To be sure, the distinction remains between what is *acceptable* and what is not, but to be acceptable does not mean "to be acceptable as true." It means "to accord with experience," rather than "to accord with the world as it really is." Science needs no more. It cannot endow with meaning the concept of truth as the conformity to things. To measure probability is not to "measure" the distance from the truth in a transcendental sense —as if we knew in advance where the truth resides to assess our distance from it (if we knew it, we would be already there, there would be no distance any more). The very task to reach the truth in the current (transcendental) sense appeared self-contradictory: to know about the world-in-itself amounts to knowing about the world which is entirely independent of the fact that it is being known, i.e. to producing a cognitive situation which does not involve the object of cognition, or a cognitive situation which is not a cognitive situation. This was roughly the result of the way in which Descartes and Hume were interpreted by German and French empiricists at the end of the 19th century, in particular by Mach and Avenarius. They argued that we could not ask about the world without encompassing the world within the very act of asking, and hence the act of asking could not be removed from the content of the question. Consequently a question related to the "independent world" could not be put at all, since the very act of questioning established interdependence. To ask about being-in-itself means to ask how to know the world without knowing it. On this view, the questions of Descartes, Locke, and Kant turned out to be wrongly formulated. Cognitive activity was supposed to reveal its real, biologically determined sense. Cognition is a certain kind of behavior of the human organism, and its function consists in restoring the equilibrium that is constantly disturbed by stimuli from the environment. The predicates "true" and "false" are not found in experience (not unlike the predicates "good" or "bad," "beautiful," or "ugly"). They belong to the human interpretation of experience. All cognitive activity, including philosophical and religious thought, has to be considered as a kind of biological reaction. Cognition is possible, and knowledge is possible—but not the theory of knowledge that would legitimate its claims to "objectivity."

*Why should we think logically?* The results of this criticism—in particular the renunciation of "truth" and "certitude" in the traditional sense—amounted, in Husserl's eyes, to the ruination of European culture. The interpretation of logic in empirical categories, or "psychologism" in logic, seemed to him especially dangerous and destructive. It was natural for him to begin from this question, since the possibility of certainty could not be decided until we know how the formal conditions for the correctness of thought are justified. How do we know that two contradictory judgments cannot be both true? Why do we believe that logical rules are valid or that our thinking *ought to* comply with them? The psychologism in its radical version consisted in the statements that logic *described* the laws of thinking, and that thinking was a psychological process. Thus logical propositions tell us how we do think. They describe regularities governing a certain realm of human behavior. *Why* we think according to these rules is either because our brains are built so that we cannot do otherwise or else because they govern our psychological processes (whatever their connection with the brain). Logic as a science is nothing other than an abstract description of empirical psychological facts.

Husserl was sure that psychologism ended in skepticism and relativism, that it made science impossible, and that it devastated the entire intellectual legacy of mankind. After Natorp, Frege, and Bolzano (who, in his opinion, had not downed the adversary consistently enough), Husserl attacked psychologism. He tried to show that the theory was self-contradictory, that it was based on the confusion of the meaning of judgments with the acts of judging, and that it utterly and absurdly distorted the sense we really ascribe to logic. To followers of psychologism, he argued, the rules of logic, far from being obligatory commands, simply state empirical facts. The consequences of thought, then, are not logical consequences of thought but causal relations between facts of our consciousness. To say that the sentence "all dogs are mammals" entails the sentence "some mammals are dogs" does not really mean that anything logically follows anything. It simply displays a causal relation between two acts of acceptance related to these two judgments. Some mysterious natural laws connect

these two acts in a causal succession of events.
Thus, logical rules are relative, if not to individuals, at least to the human species. Thus nothing
prevents us from supposing that they have no
universal validity, and they might lose it for
another sentient organism; perhaps they might
lose it for us if evolution changes some mecha-
nisms of our nervous system. Perhaps there is a
world where rational beings think according to
the principle "if p, then not-p."

What is wrong with such an idea? A lot, in
Husserl's view. There are, in his criticism, traditional antiskeptical arguments: the words "true"
and "false" have a well-defined meaning in our
language; whoever says that a judgment may be
true for one species and untrue for another one
cannot use the word "true" in its usual sense,
while at the same time attributing to his statement the value of truth in the usual sense. We
cannot retain the meanings of "true" and "false"
while denying the principle of contradiction. To
say that some thinking beings do not abide by it
means either that they think erroneously—which
happens to humans as well, and that people *in fact*
think illogically is not an argument against the
validity of logic—or that they live in a world
where "the truth" is not submitted to the principle of contradiction, which thus proves that the
word "truth" cannot there have the sense we give

it. The very concept of truth makes it impossible to say "there is no truth," for this would mean "it is true that nothing is true." However if the truth has its sources in generic qualities of man, this implies that nothing is true unless it is accepted as such; and this means precisely that there is no truth without humans—that "it is true that nothing is true." Moreover, according to the current sense of the word we must say that whatever happens, the statement that it does is true; if there is no truth, then there is no world about which the truth may be uttered; or we are forced to admit that the very existence of the world depends on the constitution of the human species. Still, people who say this, appeal to the existence of connections between our thinking and the biological facts of human evolution, and they accept these connections as true, falling again into *hysteron proteron*.

Psychologism, Husserl argues, fails to make the distinction between the meaning of judgment and the act of judging. My act of affirming the judgment that $2 + 2 = 4$ is causally determined, but it would be absurd to say that the truth of this judgment is causally determined. Otherwise we should be forced to admit that truth arises in the act of its being thought or that Pythagoras' theorem became valid only at the moment when it was uttered by Pythagoras.

And so, against psychologism, Husserl builds his program of pure logic whose validity does not depend on psychology or on any other science, on empirical facts, on the existence of human species, on the existence of the world, on causal connections, or on time. Not unlike arithmetic, logic is based on the meaning of ideal categories, employed in all domains of human knowledge. These meanings, however, do not have an ontological status similar to the Platonic ideas. In fact, their ontological status is not clear: they are neither autonomous ideal entities nor psychological acts. They make up the realm of transcendental norms in the Kantian sense. They seem to be a priori entities, valid not only for our species but containing universal rules of rationality. Both logic and mathematics deal with ideal—eternal—objects. The truth is eternal, and so are the laws of logic ("eternal" meaning not "everlasting," but "timeless"). That it is true that $2 + 2 = 4$ does not depend on whether or not there are objects to be counted; the law "either p or not-p," does not depend on whether or not there are people who think and reason. This truth is related to all possible judgments as ideal meanings. It is irrelevant to the validity of the principle of contradiction, whether or not it is psychologically possible to defy it. Even if we are built in such a way that we do in fact think in conformity with the

requirements of bivalent logic, this does not mean
that logical laws rule our consciousness. In contrast to empirical laws, the logical ones cannot be
approximate or more or less probable; they do not
risk refutation by experience, and they do not
need empirical confirmation. We know them a
priori, thanks to a peculiar sort of insight that
allows us to grasp their necessity in the very
moment of understanding them. This certitude is
not a subjective feeling (such a feeling can be
misleading and it proves nothing), it radiates from
the very meaning of judgments, it is an apodictic
certitude inhabiting this meaning. Husserl took
up the Cartesian distinction between apodictic
"evidence" and the psychological sensation of
evidence. His purpose is to combat the Protago-
rean principle stating that man is the measure of
all things, to restore the nonrelative validity of
truth, to abolish the contingency of knowledge
and its dependence on the human species.

That the laws of logic are independent of
empirical facts does not mean that they are
tautologies in the sense widely accepted in the
positivist tradition; they are not valid by virtue of
linguistic conventions (not in the sense that the
law "if p and q, then q and p" cannot be denied
without violating the meaning of the word "and,"
not unlike the sentence "all bachelors are unmarried" could be denied only by somebody who does

not understand either the word "bachelor" or the word "unmarried" or both). If the laws of logic depended on conventions of language in which they happen to be uttered, the logic could be as contingent as these very conventions. This is not how Husserl expresses his thought, but it is obviously his intention. Otherwise (i.e., if we interpreted logical laws as tautologies), it would make no sense to say that they are valid irrespective of the human species, they would be relative to the language and even to each ethnic language separately, since there is nothing like the language in general, only particular languages. And even if it is true that all known languages have common features, sedimentated as logical laws, we still remain within the generic relativity—within a sort of "human nature"—that explains nothing. The questions would remain: why do all languages compel people to think according to the same logic? Why do they all generate the same conventions? We may imagine, of course, that an answer is to be found in anthropology, that a reason for this identity will be discovered in genetic circumstances or in properties of our nervous system. But such answers, even if they come up, would not allow us to go beyond generic relativism. To Husserl it is not linguistic conventions that decide the validity of logic, but ideal meanings of concepts, and these meanings have to

be distinguished both from the objects meant and
from our acts of thinking. Husserl's critique of
psychologism carries a well-developed embryo of
his later theory of transcendental rationality. We
want to escape the extreme skepticism that reduces the laws of thought to contingent qualities
of a certain species, that destroys the objective
validity of our knowledge and that regards the
truth as a property of our behavior. Once we yield
to skepticism we deny ourselves the right to
understand the world. What remains is a contingent picture produced in the brain as result of
contingent circumstances. If we want to save the
trust in Reason, in the validity of knowledge, and
to preserve the very meaning of the concept
"truth," we must not base logic on psychological
laws. We have to find the transcendental foundation of certitude.

This was the idea which led Husserl from his
attacks on psychologism to his program of phenomenology, as a method of describing necessary
structures of the world, a method that is free from
the impact of psychological constructions. Eventu-
ally it led him to the idea of transcendental
consciousness, which constitutes these structures as
correlates of its own intentional acts—to transcendental idealism. It is important to try to grasp a
certain "logic" in the movement that started with
the struggle against psychological idealism in the

name of "objective certitude" and ended with
another kind of idealism. Whether this evolution
may be regarded as a personal accident in
Husserl's thought, or rather as the organic matu-
ration of his initial premises, this question is not
only historically, but philosophically important.

*What is convincing and what is not in the first stage of
Husserl's quest for certitude*  Are the arguments
against psychologism irrefutable? Is Husserl's idea
of pure logic clear? To be sure, we cannot base
our belief in the validity of logic on the fact that
this is how people actually think, because people
actually make logical mistakes, and even the
discovery of some human groups thinking and
speaking in defiance of the principle of contradiction would not refute this principle in our eyes.
Husserl's arguments against the statement that
logic is in fact a description of the forms of actual
human reasonings are convincing. But not so his
arguments against a Humean or Machian interpretation of logic, which does not imply that
logical laws can be proved or justified by psychological facts. Mach maintains that the concept of
truth in the current sense is useless, a relic of
metaphysical prejudices. The empirical concept of
acceptability is quite satisfactory. Science, on his
view, is a continuation of daily life reactions,
employing the same common sense criteria of

acceptability. It is a kind of socially recorded conditioned-reflex system. As any nervous system, which after a certain number of associations, spontaneously "admits" that it "pays" to establish (provisionally) certain connections as valid, so the "science," a social organ, assesses the regularities in nature. Humans have additional instruments of accumulating their knowledge and conveying it in the form of language, and logic is only an instrument making this accumulation possible; it *is* in fact relative to the language, but not to actual thought processes. "Acceptable" does not mean "admitted as true." The problem of truth on this view is indeed insoluble, not because of a mystery, but because it was wrongly put. Science can operate without it and without setting up claims to transcendental value. This interpretation is not self-contradictory or absurd in Husserl's sense, although it does not offer us an escape from relativism and it does imply the renunciation of the concept of science conceived as a better and better copy of the world-in-itself.

Husserl's critics have repeatedly noticed that his attack on psychologism made arbitrary assumptions concerning the ideal units of meaning which were not products of human thought and were independent of human psychology, biology, and history. What reasons do we have to believe in this realm of meaning? And what is the modus essendi of these entities, which are neither Plato's ideas nor psychological acts? What other reasons could we offer on their behalf except that otherwise we cannot legitimate the claims of science to "truth" in traditional sense?

Husserl, not unlike Descartes, failed to provide a clear distinction between psychological and objective certitude. He speaks of insight as a special experience, but experience is a psychological fact, and how then can we talk about meaning being independent of such facts? This special experience is no doubt supposed to discover meaning, not to produce it, but how can we assure ourselves that we have reached the proper meaning? The criteria for distinguishing two kinds of certitude are wanting. Probably it will turn out that the ultimate content of experience is not communicable. Certainly, all contents are incommunicable. But validity in human knowledge is granted only to what is communicable in language (at least in science), and the experience of certitude in Husserl's sense appears as incommunicable as a mystical experience.

Piaget's theory is a psychological interpretation of logic which resists Husserl's arguments. He tried to show how the norms of thinking were being formed, phylo- and ontogenetically, under the impact of three factors: social communication (which alone can beget the very need of proving anything, of founding one's own standpoint), practical manipulations with objects in early childhood, and language (this does not impose, as a sufficient condition, logical schemes, but makes their articulation possible). We do not know the mind as a tabula rasa, we find some cognitive schemas in earliest behavior, and the mutual pressure of these schemas and of new perceptions produces the socially accepted norms of logic. The principle of contradiction is a necessary condition of any human solidarity and of communication, and this is what makes it a universal norm of thinking. Logical rules have no validity prior to their effective constitution in social life and in thinking; they are created as forms of practical communication among people. The same may be said of arithmetic and geometric concepts. It would be silly to say according to Piaget, that "in nature itself" the solar system has nine planets; there is nothing like "nine" in nature; the "nine" as a possible property of certain systems in the world arises with the presence of "nine" in our thought, in behavior, and in language. Logic does not need to be validated in experience, but experience makes possible conceptual instruments that endow logical rules with "truth." This is, certainly, a generic relativism which has no discernible philosophical consequences in Piaget's writings. The question remains: how can we overcome generic relativism from within the conceptual framework historically produced by our species? How can we validate objective certitude without freeing ourselves from dependence on our biological and historical conditioning?

The controversy between the psychological and Husserlian interpretations of logic is the controversy between empiricism and the belief in transcendental Reason. After Leibniz, Husserl's philosophy was the strongest argument in favor of the statement that from the empiricist point of view the concept of truth is useless, and so is the concept of science as the search for truth. Adversaries of the transcendental approach do not like to accept this conclusion. When Popper argues that in the development of science we can, on empirical grounds, eliminate certain hypotheses as contrary to experience, and that such an elimination never establishes the rival hypotheses as true, he should draw the conclusion that we never are (and never will be) able to exclude the possibility that our knowledge of the world is made up entirely of false statements. However if that is so, it makes no sense to talk about the development of science as a movement closer and closer to the truth. Still, this is precisely how Popper views science. I think he is wrong in this point. I believe that whoever consistently rejects the transcendentalist idea is bound to reject not only the "absolute truth" but the truth *tout court*, not only the certitude as something already gained but the certitude as a hope as well.

It is arguable that the controversy cannot be decided with appeal to premises which the antagonists—an empiricist and a transcendentalist— would both agree to be valid. The empiricist will argue that transcendental arguments imply the existence of the realm of ideal meanings, and that we have no empirical grounds to believe in it. The transcendentalist will argue that this very argument, just advanced by the empiricist, implies the monopoly of experience as the highest tribunal of our thought, that this privileged position is precisely under question, and that it is arbitrary to establish such a monopoly. The transcendentalist compels the empiricist to renounce—for the sake of consistency—the concept of truth; the empiricist compels the transcendentalist to confess that in order to save the belief in Reason, he is in duty bound to admit a kingdom of beings (or quasi-beings) he cannot justify. This was Husserl's great merit: to lead this discussion to the extreme point.

# SECOND LECTURE: THE MEANS

*The need to go beyond doubt*   Husserl's strictures of psychologism are based on the presumption that our thought has no guarantee of reaching "the things" unless we achieve an absolutely original insight that fulfills two conditions. First, it must be independent of the fact that "I," the knowing subject, am a psychological person, involved in social and historical conditions, and biologically determined. Second, it must not only reach "facts" but give access to universal truth—something that is not only *hic et nunc* but reveals "necessary" connections in the world. These two postulates are expressed in Husserl's two slogans: "back to the things themselves," and "philosophy should be a rigorous science." The first slogan contains two, more specific, requirements: first, we should assure ourselves that the truth we gain is independent of philosophical prejudices and artificial abstractions, and is rooted in an absolutely primordial insight; second, nothing may be accepted unless it is founded in this primordial insight, and this is the calling of philosophy—to reveal the meaning of all particular sciences. Philosophy has to be autonomous—free from presuppositions—and it must not accept any ready-made results of science. If philosophers imagine they may "generalize" these results, they have to accept them as they are, and thus they renounce the self-critical radicalism which is

needed if the task of philosophy—to reconstruct
human knowledge as a whole—is to be realized. A
meaningful understanding of knowledge cannot
spring from its accumulation in particular sciences. The growing mass of facts, theories, hypotheses, and classifications that allows us to
predict events and improve our technology, does
not really help us in understanding the world.
While increasing his power over nature, man
extends the distance between his technological
skill and his capacity to understand. The sciences
measure things without realizing what they measure; in carrying out cognitive acts, they are
incapable of grasping these very acts. They cannot spontaneously produce their own meaning
and justify their aspirations to objectivity. In
particular Husserl criticizes three intellectual attitudes which either do not grasp or explicitly reject
the "proper" epistemological question (in the
Kantian sense). The first target is *naturalism*,
regarding consciousness as an object in the world,
to be investigated psychologically. Within this
attitude we may analyze the contents of consciousness, but it does not enable us to ask about
its validity (that we distinguish illusions from
"correct" perceptions is epistemologically irrelevant, since experimental psychology provides no
criteria to show that the "correct" perceptions
really reach the things). The second target is

*historicism*, in which we analyze knowledge as a product of human history, as a set of facts of culture. In doing this we relativize cognitive contents as we view them in changing historical situations, we interpret them genetically, and we set aside the distinction between science as a cultural fact and science as valid or invalid knowledge, and we cancel science as an object of epistemological evaluation. The third target is the *Weltanschauungsphilosophie*, in Dilthey or in other versions. It considers philosophy as an expression of personal, social, or historical values, which are valid for a particular period or for a particular human community. It cannot establish (nor does it want to) that something is a real value (cognitive or other), regardless of its period, of its community, of the person. In defiance of scientism, positivism, and relativism—all these are germs of the dissolution of European culture—Husserl looks for a method that would justify the claims of knowledge to a validity independent of history, persons, society, or biological circumstance. He looks for criteria that keep the same virtue whether or not the world exists.

Thus philosophy has purposely to neglect the existing body of knowledge as a whole: the reality science presents is either mediated through theories or known only as a stream of subjective perceptions that can be always suspected of being just products of a personal psyche. Philosophy must neglect all the evidence of daily life. It rejects all beliefs of the natural attitude that accepts the world as an unquestionable datum and is unable to face the problems of existence and validity.

But there *is* an original insight where things reveal themselves to the consciousness directly, "bodily," undistorted. It is neither common perception, with its underlying beliefs, nor analytical knowledge. Phenomenology wants to offer us access to such an insight, to investigate essential significant structures—connections in the world which are not simply empirically perceived but are apodictically necessary, irrespective of actual experience. To elaborate such a method, we cannot rely on the empirio-critical concept of the ontological neutrality of experience; we cannot simply state that elements of experience are neither reflections of things nor combinations of psychological contents. We cannot accept this concept for three reasons. First, it does not solve the problem of validity but simply cancels it as meaningless. Second, it reduces the notion of truth to the pragmatic one or replaces it with the notion of acceptability as defined by practical needs. Third, it admits that scientific theories describe relatively constant regularities in experience, but that they do not and they must not pretend to discover any immanent necessity. And so, the certitude is not gained but flatly removed as a problem.

Consequently, we should start our reconstruction of meaning and of the world by putting aside all results of science, all empirical facts as "given" within the world, our own "ego," and the very existence of the world and of other persons. All this may be questioned. What cannot?

*The way toward unmediated insight* To answer this, Husserl enters the path of Descartes and takes up his reasoning with some—important—modification. I cannot start with the belief in the transcendent existence of the world as it appears. However the fact that my perceptions are such and such, this fact is given in the absolute sense. The contents of my actual *cogitationes* (in the all-embracing Cartesian sense) are given me originally, immanently, undeniably, ignorant though I am about the nature of *cogitata* (objects) or of the thinking subject. We deal with phenomena, qualities whose mode of being is not directly "given." The pure phenomenon of my perceiving, judging, experiencing, and willing can be the object of a direct insight; it is immanently present, here. We may describe it *as* it appears without deciding what it is, but still we may hope that in *how* it appears we will discover some constitutive, necessary qualities of the world.

And so we imitate Descartes in that we do not see anything obvious in the fact of the existence of the world. However Descartes' blunder consists in his decision that he could doubt the existence of the world but not his own existence—that his Ego was given him in absolute immediacy and he was thus a thinking substance. But in pure phenomena no thinking substance appears. Therefore we have to eliminate the substantial Ego as well. Such a purification of the field of consciousness from any existence—this transcendental reduction—is the first and necessary operation on the way toward certitude. It frees me from all prejudices of common sense, in particular concerning the existence of both the world and the subject. Both are suspended or put into brackets or endowed with the "epistemological zero-indicator." We neither negate their existence nor even doubt it, we simply put the question provisionally aside. We suspend any transcendence, anything going beyond the pure phenomenon of *cogitatio*. This phenomenon *is* given, but not so the fact that it is "mine," that it belongs to an empirical person. Neither is the fact given that a phenomenon "represents" an object. (The difference from the Kantian concept of phenomenon is unmistakable: to Kant, the phenomenon is an appearance *of* something; that phenomena revealed things was to him obvious, direct; we do

not know how the thing is in itself, but we do
know immediately that it is revealed in the
phenomenon; as if—though Kant does not say
so—the existence of things was an analytical
truth, included in the very sense of the word
"phenomenon." This is not implied in Husserl's
concept, existence being excluded from acceptable
immediacy). All alleged evidence, all realities of
daily life—external bodies, my own body, my self
(as a part of the world), constructions of physical,
social, and mathematical sciences, all these are
cancelled for the time being. Within such a
purified field, I know neither the world nor
consciousness as belonging to it, I know only
phenomena as intentional correlates of my conscious acts. The world before and after the
reduction does not differ in content, only in my
attitude, in the meaning of "transcendence"
which I used to attribute to it. (The terms
"transcendental reduction" and "epoché" can be
dealt with as equivalents; the later distinction
between them is unimportant here).

The very term "transcendental" is not suf-
ficiently explained in Husserl's writing. At one
point he says that the reduction is transcendental
—which means that it cancels the belief in
transcendence. In most contexts saying that
knowledge is transcendental means precisely that
its validity is independent of the fact, that it is

experienced, accepted or not, by biologically, psychologically, historically, socially defined subjects. Thus the function of the reduction is both negative (it clears *cogitationes* from prejudices about transcendence) and positive (it gives access to transcendental consciousness).

What remains after the reduction are the contents of phenomena *and* the place where they appear, or the transcendental, not nonempirical Ego, the pure subject of cognition, the recipient of phenomena, something having none of the properties usually attributed to psychological subjects, and retaining, nevertheless, the intentional relation to its object. The *act* of cogitatio and its *content, noesis* and *noēma,* have to be distinguished, but they are both only given together. An object is an object only to the Ego, the Ego is always directed toward an object.

The world, so reduced on both sides, can be investigated and can reveal to us the secret of the meaning of our knowledge. Within it we also may start reconstructing the world of values (as phenomena). The dichotomy of facts and values, of descriptive and value judgments, is cancelled. After the reduction they are equalized as phenomena: "red color" is as good a phenomenon as "love" or "sacrifice." The dichotomy is inescapable from the empiricist standpoint, as is the question of how values may be inferred from facts, but in the phenomenal world—after suspension of ontological questions—it vanishes. So phenomenology promises to overcome not only epistemological but ethical relativism.

The reduction seems to be conceived as provisional; we decide neither on the reality of the world nor on its priority over consciousness, yet we do not say in advance that these problems cannot come back or that they are insoluble or meaningless. The question remains open, whether and how what we achieve within the phenomenal world will appear to be valid for the "real" world. Briefly, we leave open the possibility that the "brackets" will be taken away. However we should ask if it is true, if, within Husserl's program, we will ever be allowed to take off the brackets without crossing out the results of the reduction.

Thus the direct intuition or the unshakable evidence to which such a reduction gives us access seems at the start limited in its aspirations; but it soon turns out that its aspirations are limitless. We uncover, Husserl maintains, a new unquestionable sphere of being (pure phenomena) where nothing is excluded from inquiry and where everything gives certainty. We describe phenomena as they appear, and we try to grasp their structures. Our descriptions, though apodictic, are never complete and similar in this to "natural,"

naïve perception, but they enable us to see
directly such connections of things that once we
grasp them, we *know* that it cannot be otherwise—
we really hold the necessity. Descartes, although
on the threshold of transcendental subjectivity,
did not reach it. He decided that the substantial
Ego is what resists all doubts and he retained it as
an intact piece of the "natural" world. Once we
remove even this piece, we deal with meaning, of
which the world-reference is unknown and not
asked. The world appears as the phenomenon of
the world.

*Doubts about transcendental reduction*   Is such a
suspension of existence practicable and what does
it imply? Husserl is right in saying that Descartes
tried to save ego as something from the world, as
an irreducible remainder, and that he provisionally took the solipsist standpoint. This is what
Husserl objects to him: We ought to exclude all
existence in order to reach radical insight. Do we
understand what that means? It may be argued,
as Kant did, that existence is not a real predicate,
at least when related to the world as a whole. To
carry out the reduction we first have to understand what the existence of the world (including
ego) means in the absolute sense. Do we? When
we ask whether a thing exists, we ask whether it
belongs to the world, whether it is a part of the

world. We grasp existence only as belonging to the world. This is why the meaning of the question, "does everything exist? (including the subject)" is utterly obscure. When we deprive everything of the predicate of existence, nothing (it seems) changes, nothing at all. It seems that we understand the so-called controversy about the existence of the world only in the Cartesian sense, we understand at the very outmost the question of solipsism, but once I remove myself as empirical Ego, the question loses meaning. One cannot rationally ask whether everything exists. The world, Husserl says, may be a consistent dream. Perhaps. I vaguely imagine what it does mean as long as I imagine myself as dreaming. When I am no longer the dreaming subject, I cannot see how to express the difference between the world as a dream and the world as real. This is why it is extremely dubious that the reduction opens a new realm of being to us.

Moreover, we do not know what the transcendental Ego, remaining after the reduction, really is. Nor is it clear why the word "Ego" is used. This is not a part of the world, Husserl says, this is not me, a human person knowing itself in the "natural" experience. This distinction between psychological and transcendental Ego (the latter being a pure unpsychological subject of cognition), when we repeat it often enough, begins ultimately to

seem intelligible. But this is an illusory intelligibil-
ity. The transcendental Ego is an empty recipient
of cognitive content and nothing else, a place
where phenomena appear. Husserl perhaps experienced this kind of reduction of himself, but in
order that a method be of value, it has to be
capable of being handed over to others. The word
"Ego" is misleading. To say "I exists" is ungram-
matical, and so is the saying "the I exists" since
"I" is a pronoun and not a noun; it is as simple as
that. We avoid the difficulty by using a latin word
"Ego," but this is a verbal trick.

Certainly, many investigations can be, and in
fact are, pursued in all the sciences without asking
questions about the ontological status of the
objects. But this is not what Husserl means, since
such investigations cannot bring us any certitude.
The ontological question is simply neglected and
not consciously put out of mind along with a
careful purification of the field of perception. It
seems that the pursuit of certitude should imply,
in Husserl's view, the explicit statement that
certitude excludes all existential prejudices. And
the question arises: What is this certitude about,
and how can it be communicated?

*The search for universals*   The answer lies in the
next step of the Husserlian method, eidetic reduction. If the description of a phenomenon grasped

only its actual hic et nunc, we would have a
certitude, but this certitude would be scientifically
worthless. The task of phenomenology is not to
describe a singular phenomenon but to uncover in
it the universally valid and scientifically fruitful
essence, or *eidos*. The eidetic insight, however, is
not a procedure of abstraction, but a special kind
of direct experience of universals, which reveal
themselves to us with irresistible self-evidence. We
do not presuppose any separate, autonomous
kingdom of ideas, and we remain within transcendental consciousness. Still, our insight is irreducible to singular perceptions and so is its *noēma*; we
do not simply generalize, abstract, or neglect some
sides of objects to extract the universal. Husserl
rejects the traditional empiricist theory of abstraction, which implies that direct experience always
deals with singularity, while the process of abstraction is nothing but an economizing symbolic
notation purported to record some actually important common qualities of many objects. Such a
theory implies that any abstraction is as good as
any other, that each concept is properly built if it
can be applied to the purpose for which it was
created, and that all criteria of selecting qualities
are equally correct and all produce a sort of
practically useful distortion. This theory implies
in addition that knowledge of universals does not
add anything to the experience of individuals, it

has no autonomous cognitive value, and it does not reveal in the world anything that would not be included in particular perceptions.

To Husserl, on the contrary, universals are not inferred from individuals but are given directly, "bodily." Thus his concept is opposed to the Platonic realism (which accepts a separate transcendent world of universals), to the theory of universals *in re* (implying that the essence is a quality of a transcendent object), to the conceptualist interpretation (accepting "universality" as a property of mind), and to nominalism (which considers universality as a property of language, a *loquendi modus*) Husserl's specific approach presupposes his concept of transcendental subject. An eidos reveals itself in a particular object, but the object appears only as a correlate of the intentional act, without being its arbitrary construction. Thus the eidos does not go beyond the subject. Without the experience of essence, no meaning and no meaningful judgments would be possible; whatever we say of objects—real or imaginary—we intend a "species being." In saying "this stone is grey" we do not mean a particular greyness but a genus greyness, and this genus is immediately given. A nominalist would say, of course, that we are dealing with a similarity of objects in some respects and that we grasp this similarity in abstract predicates. This is false, according to Husserl. The actual object of such judgments (or their meaning) is not an individual greyness. We cannot state the similarity without knowing *previously* in respect of what the objects are similar, and then we have to do not with the similarity but with identity (as being simply grey, all grey stones are identical). A nominalist says that such concepts originated in acts of comparison, but for Husserl, first, the genetical question is epistemologically irrelevant and second, the very acts of comparison imply the presence of essences. And so when empiricists argue that we confront similarities of things in different respects, we should ask: What makes it that this and that similarity are both similarities? The answer is their similarity to the genus similarity. (This characteristically Platonic reasoning—the similarity is what makes things similar—is in fact not far from Russell's approach to the problem of universals, in particular in the "Inquiry into Meaning and Truth.") The main argument seems to be that we would be incapable of producing conceptual categories based on similarity, if we did not previously know the genus "similarity." Consequently there is similarity, not only similar objects. What is true for perception is a fortiori true for ideal mathematical objects.

Thus the essences, though they appear only within the insights of individuals, of examples, are irreducible to individuals; they are timeless and spaceless (the phenomenon of time itself is timeless, too—it does not contain the real time). Even in grasping an object *as* an individual we imply that we conceive it as a particularization of something universal, and so the individuality itself, when it is the object of our intention, shows the eidos. It is in the perception itself that we catch the meaning of "being red," and there are no things which would be red "in general," since redness has many shades. The same applies to grasping the meaning of "being colored," and no object is colored in general. And so it is with perceiving the fact that whatever is colored is extended: this is not an anlytical sentence, nor a linguistic compulsion. Once we say this, we know that it cannot be otherwise and that we recognize a necessity of things themselves, this necessity being valid irrespective of whether or not real things exist. We do not need many examples to get universal and necessary knowledge of this kind, and this knowledge does not spring from their accumulation; nor do we need to know that there is anything real corresponding to these objects.

We aim to find out the necessary structures of universals, to establish the qualities that necessarily belong to them, so that if they were lost the object would lose its identity. In what Husserl calls "the free imaginary variation" we try to imagine the object (a universal), while neglecting or mentally exchanging some of its properties, and so we conclude that some of them, even if they empirically always accompany the phenomenon, do not structurally belong to it, and their absence leaves the nature of phenomenon untouched; while others cannot be abolished without the identity of the phenomenon being abolished with it. This operation deals with things (phenomena) as meaningful, not with the conventional senses of words. Therefore the results appear not in the form of analytical judgments but as phenomenological eidetic description. We may analyze connections of all sorts among structures (their similarity, analogy, dependence, mutual dependence, formal–ontological priority, etc.) and so build many eidetic sciences corresponding to particular empirical and deductive disciplines. They will explain and describe the original meaning of the basic concepts of any given science (like the concept of number in mathematics or the concept of the work of art in art history) without presupposing any actual achievements of any existing science. This is what may provide particular sciences with the self-awareness of their own operations; they will understand what they are actually dealing with. Such a phenomenological "structuration" of the conceptual apparatus of science is not arbitrary, Husserl believes. It does

not define ready made terms or take up existing
conceptual schemas and classifications. It conveys
to us significant structures of which the meaning-
fulness or the teleological order are imposed
neither by conventions nor by psychological circumstances ("I cannot think it otherwise"), but
radiate from the object with imperative self-
evidence.

*The desire for immediacy versus the desire for being
scientific*   Thus is the sense of the slogan "back to
things themselves" revealed. It means "back to
universals," but to universals that are not produced arbitrarily or for the sake of convenience
and do not make up a separate realm of being; it
means, "back to universals as direct objects of
intellectual intuition." We want to know whether
our science and our common sense cut the world
according to its, as it were, "natural" fibers or
according to our practical needs and conventions
(a difference which cannot be done within phe-
nomenalism and empiricism), whether or not
scientific concepts are correctly and meaningfully
built (in conformance with necessary properties of
eidetic structures). Husserl is a Platonist insofar as
he believes in the natural classification of things.
But this kind of inquiry does not properly belong
to any particular science. (The history of art deals
with works of art but the analysis of what the

work of art in general is and must be, goes beyond
its tasks; causal relations are studied in all sciences, but the eidos of causality in none of them.)

No object is excluded in advance from such an
inquiry; we may pile up and classify phenomena
infinitely. My intuition might be vague, but I can
direct my attention toward vagueness as a property of my intuition and get at a clear insight of
vagueness, and then I can study the act of perception as vague, and then the clear act of
perception directed toward vagueness and so on.
And everything depends ultimately on the quality
of the original insight in which things reveal
themselves. We aim at nonanalytical certitude.
How can we assure ourselves that we have a
genuine certitude? Phenomenology provides no
answer: either you have insight or you do not.
And then the question arises: How this certitude
can be communicated? In trying to answer, we
come across a clash between the two basic slogans
of phenomenology: "back to things themselves"
and "philosophy should be a rigorous science."
That an inquiry is rigorous implies that it can be
communicated: we must be able to convey its
content in words so that whoever understands us
reaches the same certitude. This is not the case
with phenomenology. Certitude is in the act of
insight, not in discourse. The task of phenomenology is to describe a certain peculiar sphere of

experience, and the description cannot replace the experience; at best it can make it easier for another person to achieve a similar insight. The same may of course be said of any direct experience. Qualitative content is not symbolically communicable, but that is precisely why qualitative description cannot pretend to be "rigorous science."

*Is there anything wrong with eidetic reduction?* The trouble with Husserl's method is that his writings give very few examples of it. A "rigorous" method is one that, whenever applied will lead every person to (approximately) the same result. But how can we ascertain ourselves that it is so? Certainly, many phenomenologists tried to apply the "method," not simply to describe it. Eidetic description is universally applicable; we may describe the eidos of the color red, of the relation of similarity, of architecture, the state, religion, love, moral value, social bonds, and our acts of seeing each of these objects. We may, for example, reflect on the "eidos" of religion: does the belief in personal deity make up its necessary part? Or is it the existence of a religious organization, the belief in afterlife, or the experience of "the Holy"? There are no reasons to presume that everyone will arrive at the same conclusions, and if one says "I have had the insight, you haven't," the discus-

sion must come to a stop. For Husserl, the
ultimate material of knowledge is not communicable, but what is communicable is of great
significance; the skill of a phenomenologist does
not consist in remembering ready made truths but
in a constant effort to purify one's own consciousness from naïve stereotypes and beliefs of daily
life, from the apparent evidence of science, from
habitual and misleading concepts or from the
blurring of the distinction between the facts of
experience and its content.

Still, what is of great value in Husserl's teach-
ing—his radical self-criticism, his courage in
going obstinately back to the beginnings—is not
enough to support his belief that he discovered a
reliable method of reaching nonanalytical certainty. Let us take from Husserl the simplest
example of a necessary synthetic truth, "what is
colored is extended." It seems that this is not an
accidental association. Once we know what
"color" is, we immediately know that it cannot be
otherwise, that there are no colored numbers or
feelings. But in what sense is our knowledge a
priori? A skeptic may argue that once we produce
the concept of color, it is obviously only applicable
to surfaces and thus the sentence just quoted *is* an
analytical judgment, not unlike the sentence
"every triangle has three sides." Another example,
"orange is between red and yellow," is supposed

to be apodictically evident. Why? The word
"between" originally described a topological relation. If we split light into the spectrum, or if we
watch the rainbow, orange is topologically "between" red and yellow—but this is strictly empirical. In another sense the statement can mean that
we get orange when we mix yellow and red paint,
but again, there is nothing a priori in this. I *may*
deny that the statement is apodictically obvious.
A phenomenologist, in such a case, can only
answer that I am stupid and that is the end of the
dispute.

It is arguable that many of Husserl's remarks to
the effect that in our perception and imagination
we "directly" grasp something universal are well
founded. Perhaps the sense of this universality is
different from what he thought. The idea that
there are atomic perceptions out of which concepts are subsequently extracted has been often
criticized, not only from the phenomenological
point of view (in Gestalt psychology, e.g.). It is
convincing to say that a "meaning," consequently
a "universal," makes itself part of the perception:
A baby does not *see* the same thing that an adult
does when it "looks" at objects and is ignorant of
their function and place in the purposeful order;
an adult perceives objects as endowed with meaning, and he does not *add* the meaning to his
perceptions; when I see a car, I *see* a car and not a
colored surface that I interpret separately as part

of a purposely organized universe; when I look at
a text in an alphabet unknown to me I do not *see*
what a person who can read it does, and I do not
perceive differences that he sees directly, his
understanding of the text converges with his
seeing into one single act. Everyone agrees that
perception is selective, because it is under pressure
from biological and social circumstances. This
does not entail that we experience essences, only
that our experience is culturally conditioned, by
language among other factors. How, for example,
could we reflect upon the eidos of religion or of
causal relationship "without presuppositions," so
that the results of our reflection would be valid,
regardless of whether or not any religion exists?
We can try to fix the "essence" only on the
condition that we have hold of—even in a vague
form—the meaning of the phenomenon as it was
conveyed in language. And this means, as we take
it from collective experience. Language divides
the world in a certain way, and our perception no
doubt would be different without it, but once we
decide to start analyzing the "essence" of something, we have always to deal with the sedimenta-
tion of secular experiences of mankind and these
experiences, though historically explainable, do
not carry any logical necessity. Consequently,
certain resources of common sense are inevitably
present in acts which make up the phenomenolog-

ical method; there are unremovable residuals of common sense in any experience; while performing the transcendental reduction we cannot get rid of language, and this means: of the whole cultural history of mankind. It seems hardly possible, as Husserl appears to believe, that we could go back to the intellectual innocence of a newborn baby and still remain phenomenologists. Since there are such residuals in our minds, we have no guarantee at all against illusions, in other words, we have no source of certitude. I cannot have a phenomenological insight without being able to give a name to the object of my insight.

An additional danger of Husserl's method consists in that it allows us entirely to dispense with learning history. No "essence" will spring from piling up examples. To produce a general phenomenological theory of the novel it is enough to have read one novel, to build a universal theory of religion we do not need to know more than one religion. This is perhaps one of the reasons why phenomenology does not seem to have contributed to making inquiries in human sciences "more rigorous"; instead, it made free speculation easier.

Husserl certainly posed questions of paramount importance to the humanities: How do we know that our concepts are properly built? Is our "cutting" of the world arbitrary, guided by practical considerations, or does it fit in the "real" network of relations? As long as we are unable to answer such questions we do not know what, if anything, our thought grasps or whether it is more than a practical instrument. Still, we have no universally valid criteria to catch meaningful structures. The need for such criteria has been strongly felt in the humanities and has resulted in many attempts, dependent or not on phenomenology. The trouble is that for these questions everybody has a different insight which itself proves that we are far from apodictic certitude. It would be fair to say that the destiny of Husserl's project was similar to that of Descartes: His *pars destruens* turned out to be stronger and more convincing than his belief to have discovered an original well of certitude. This seems to be the common lot of philosophers.

# THIRD LECTURE
# THE ACHIEVEMENTS

*How the world can be the same yesterday and today*
Within transcendental reduction, everything gets
a meaning emanating from consciousness, but the
difference between act and content (or noesis and
noēma), like the difference between subject and
object, is not abrogated. On the contrary, an
essential property of conscious acts is their intentionality: they are directed toward an object
(seeing is seeing something, a desire has an object
desired, and the same applies to perceptions,
volitions, emotions, hopes, and judgments). Bren-
tano, who defined psychological phenomena (in
contrast to physical ones) as intentional, was
incapable, in Husserl's view, of abandoning the
psychological approach because he failed to distinguish the psychological Ego from the transcendental one.

The category of intentionality is fundamental
to Husserl's description of conscious acts because
only as intentional can consciousness identify the
object as being the same in many acts, which
amounts to grasping its meaning. Once we presuppose, as did Hume and Mach, that each
perception is atomlike and punctiform, and that
we produce "objects" for practical reasons, sepa-
rating some more-or-less lasting qualities out from
the stream of impressions, we are bound to accept
their conclusions: that our idea of the identity of
an object may be genetically explained, yet not

empirically justified. Then the illusion of the
identity of a thing emerges from the fact that some
relatively durable sets of qualities are sedimentated in language (hence the meaningless concept
of "substance" or of *vinculum substantiale*). We
cannot escape such a conclusion if we fail to
distinguish acts from contents, if we treat properties of the object as being real elements of consciousness (as we do in psychological idealism).
Indeed, once we fall victim to this confusion, no
element of content (and this means, the act of my
actual experience) can ever appear again: otherwise we should presume that we can reverse time.
We may, from this standpoint, accept the similarity of qualities, but it would be nonsense to talk
about the identity of an object; this would mean
that we would assert the identity of two or more
psychological acts performed at various moments
in time. But if we are careful not to neglect the
distinction just mentioned, we can save the com-
monsense belief that the stone I am seeing now is
the same stone I saw a minute ago, and not only
that these two perceptions have similar qualities.
This identity is valid after reduction—after we
suspended the belief in the "transcendence" of
objects. However what matters to Husserl is the
identity less of physical objects and more of ideal
ones, like universals, mathematical and logical
concepts, and ideal meanings. Again, without

being able to save their identity, we are not
entitled to support any claim to "objectivity" and
certainty of knowledge. There is no number that
is always the same in many acts of counting and
that is independent of them; there are only
singular acts of counting, and they do not refer to
anything identical. Each noema (or content) is
singular, but many noemata may refer to the
same numerically single object, grasped in different acts (of perceiving, judging, remembering,
feeling, and so on). This, however, is possible only
if perception is not punctiform, if every intentional act contains the actually perceived, temporal continuity of experience. Every cogito, when it
moves toward the *cogitatum,* is not as a tabula rasa,
but as an act of synthesis, which ties raw data in
the continuous world of phenomena. Internal
time-consciousness is the "form of synthesis"; and
it is through this that I grasp the object not as a
part of consciousness but as an objective meaning.
This is the inalienable feature of intentional
operations: that each subjective process has a
"horizon of reference." Any actual experience
includes *really* the *potential* one and this both in
temporal and in spatial aspects of things. When I
see a thing, my intention is directed toward
not-perceived aspects. That an object has "the
rear side" is not an intellectual assertion but an
actual element of the movement of intention. The

same has to be said of time aspects: within the intention itself there is the *retention*, a horizon of the past, an experience of the backward-facing continuity, and there is the *protention*—the anticipation of the thing as of the future one. There is no time-punctiform cogitatio, no perception limited to the pure actuality; each is stretching forward and backward beyond the field of actuality. This is what reveals an object as being the same. Consequently, this is what makes us able to find out the meaning and the reference of the object to the eidos (no eidetic reduction would be practicable without intentional synthesis).

And thus has the second blunder of Descartes been uncovered. Descartes not only wrongly believed to have had direct access to the substantial Ego, conceived as a part of the world, but he believed, no less wrongly, that a *nonintentional cogito* was possible, that he could observe his own consciousness as a pure act of cognitatio without cogitatum. For intentional analysis, however, there is no pure act of cogito without an object. And since we performed the reduction, the priceless conquest of this method, the cogitatum is given *as directly* as the cogito. We did not abolish the object, but we did abolish *any mediation* between act and object (owing to its reduction to the status of phenomenon). The identity of the object, consequently, appears with the same certitude as the identity of the transcendental Ego.

*The world as an achievement of consciousness*   However it turns out soon that the intentional movement of consciousness not only identifies objects but constitutes them as well. Here we approach the controversial topic of the meaning of the standpoint Husserl himself called "transcendental idealism." (I say "controversial" since there are commentators who do not think that we have to do with idealism in an ontological sense; most however refer to Husserl's utterances which are so unequivocal as have, in this respect, no other sense). Still, the concept of constitution remains vague: it is not a creation ex nihilo; rather it is an act of endowing the world with meaning. In transcendentally reduced consciousness, however, each act of reaching the object *is* an act of supplying it with meaning; any sense is the product of constitution, including, in particular, the sense of an object as an *existing* one. "Existence" itself is a certain "sense" of an object. Consequently it would be absurd, for Husserl, to say that an object "exists" independently of the meaning of the word "to exist"—independently of the act of constitution performed by the consciousness.

The question is whether the passage to idealism
was rooted in the very starting point of Husserl's
philosophy, or (as many realistically disposed
phenomenologists believe) it was a result of the
philosopher's personal evolution, which could
have gone another way. (Ingarden, among others,
maintained that the very principles of phenomenology, as outlined in the *Logical Investigations* do
not entail at all the idealist conclusion but are
perfectly compatible with the realist position).
Phenomenology can certainly be, and in fact was,
defined in various ways. For Husserl, however, it
included transcendental reduction. So we may
ask: Is the reduction really ontologically neutral?
Is it only a method, or does it, as a method, decide
ontological questions? Is it reversible? Will the
attempt to found the objectivity of knowledge
(and values) in locating them within transcendental subjectivity, will it ever permit us to take off
the provisory brackets from the transcendent
world? Will not these brackets appear to be
eternal fetters, tying forever the world with the
reduced subject?

To be sure, there is no theory of constitution in
the *Logical Investigations*. It may be argued nevertheless that the passage to idealism from 1907
onwards (the Göttingen lectures), without being a
logical conclusion from the early theory of meaning, was the only consistent solution to the same

problem which these early writings began to face. The theory of constitution implies that any being has validity only so far as it gains meaning in the acts of transcendental consciousness. The very concept of an absolute, self-supporting reality, not related to consciousness, is absurd and self-contradictory. Objects are sedimentations ("achievements," rather than "products") of creative acts of consciousness, the latter being the ultimate source of their crystallized shape. From this moment on, the "provisory" brackets imposed on the problem of existence become an undestructible wall.

How did it happen? By virtue of what logic did Husserl, starting with attacks on subjectivism (in the sense of relativism, irrationalism, the concept of truth as relative to consciousness), come to the conclusion that "objectivity" could only be achieved within transcendental consciousness, that *no rationalism was possible* unless based on consciousness as the only one self-grounding reality? I think that his development, far from being an accidental aberration, was very consistent and it can be reconstructed as follows:

Skepticism and relativism can be overcome only if we discover the source of absolute certitude. This certitude can be gained where we do not need to worry about "the bridge" from perceptions to things, where there is an *absolute immediacy*, where the act of cognition and its

content are *not mediated* in any way (even if their
distinction remains valid), where we simply *cannot
ask how we know* that our acts reach the content as
it *really is*—where the content is absolutely trans-
parent to the subject or is immanent. Thus
rationality and certitude may be found only if
subjectivity is not a "reflection" of objects (if it is,
the problem of the bridge remains as insoluble as
ever) but constitutes them. Only as it is dependent
on the cognitive acts, is the object accessible in a
way which makes doubt impossible. In the course
of time Husserl repeats for transcendental consciousness all the traditional arguments of empirical idealism, from Fichte to Avenarius.

After reduction, the world is a meaning, things
and other people are constituted phenomena; the
predicates "existing" and "nonexisting" refer to
what is meant and *only as such*. The predicates
"true" and "false" refer to acts of intention. The
property of existing or not existing is correlated
with acts of verification and nullification based on
insight. On the basis of this insight, the object is
"immediately intuited," is "given *originaliter*," or
given in the mode "itself there." It keeps its
identity; I can go back to it. The world is not
what is actually perceived, it is an infinite potentiality, but a potentiality of consciousness. The Ego
is not a substance, it is actual only as directed
toward something; the Ego is known only as the

"substratum" of acts, but Ego and object together have no other name, which encompasses them both, than transcendental consciousness.

In this decisive argument, all the old idealist patterns recur (and Husserl does not seem to notice): there is no truth independent of the knowledge of truth; but the saying "this or that happens" is equivalent to the saying "it is true that this or that happens," consequently to say that something happens independently of the consciousness means that a judgment can be meaningful and true, irrespective of whether there is a consciousness—which is absurd, since meaning, and truth a fortiori, are relative to the consciousness, and so is any possible object of truth. Whatever we can talk about meaningfully, is meaningful (a possible object of an utterance), and therefore to say that a certain object is independent of the possibility of uttering a judgment on it, amounts to saying that we are talking about something we are not talking about—an obvious contradiction. Ultimately everything goes back to a version of the traditional tautologies: "we cannot think about something that is not being thought"; "nothing can be an object of a judgment that is not an object of a judgment." Once we talk about something, we make it an object of judgment, thus "to be independent of the consciousness" is a self-contradictory concept.

Husserl came to conclude (consistent within his view) that "realism" is self-contradictory, and if we cancel consciousness, we cancel the world, and that consciousness alone can have a self-supporting existence.

This traditional reasoning does not end in relativism precisely because Husserl believed to have discovered a consciousness which is not *in* the world (is not a part of it) but is entirely independent of empirical consciousness, the empirical world, human psychology, biology, and history. The insight that this consciousness provides is liberated from all ties with the world. Certainly we should always say that in Husserl's view what is related "to me" is existence "for me" (this was the reason why some critics questioned Husserl's idealism, as if he was not talking about existence in general but only about existence "for me"), but I am not allowed to talk meaningfully about existence without implying the existence "for me." This is why the reduction is not a temporary suspension which we might hope to abrogate later. It prevents me forever from talking about the being that is not related to consciousness; indeed it makes utter nonsense of such a concept. There is no way back from reduction except for the return to naïve, "natural," and "uncritical" attitudes, which cannot carry any certitude. Once we begin the quest for certitude, we cannot go back without nullifying all results of the reduction. There is no logical possibility of founding a nonidealist epistemology within the phenomenological project.

Husserl, in contrast to Kant, believed that the transcendental conditions of knowledge encompass everything, both the form and the content of perception. There is no dualism of contingent *hyle* and rational organizing forms. The constitution is all-embracing, and there is no facticity or contingency left over. Still, Ego has no existence independent of its having objects: it somehow constitutes itself while constituting objects. It keeps its identity, and it can go back to its earlier perceptions (it is even called the "substratum" of its properties, but the meaning of this word in Husserl's context is obscure). In the search for cognitive necessity, we find consciousness as the only necessary being, the only *causa sui*, and this is because only consciousness is absolutely "given" to itself.

This reasoning reveals the destiny of all attempts to reach absolute certainty. Writings on Husserl often emphasize that his concept of insight has nothing to do with Bergson's intuition, that it is Cartesian rather than mystical. The difference appears obvious from first glance. For Bergson intuition is a kind of intellectual auscultation that brings us into the "interior" of the object and allows us to commune with what is unique, consequently inexpressible in the object; it is an act in which consciousness identifies with an object which previously was entirely "outside" and independent of it. No such intuition may appear in Husserl. But there is a more profound affinity between them, not only in their goal (to gain perfect certainty) but in their procedures as well. For both philosophers it turns out that *ultimate certitude can be achieved only in immanence* and that the ultimate content of this certitude is *incommunicable*. To achieve certitude I have to have an insight consisting in a perfect, unmediated convergence of act and content. The insight cannot be replaced by a verbal message which by definition is a mediating device. And so, in Bergson and Husserl intuition has the basic features of a mystical experience and is just as incommunicable. Husserl's rationalism is mystical because whatever is communicable in words is mediated, and certitude is based on the fact that to the consciousness its own act and its content cannot be subjected to doubt (as may everything else). Though the distinction of noesis and noema remains, the cogitata have only as much certitude as the cogito has.

Idealism cannot be criticized on its own presuppositions. Husserl says that as long as we keep staying in the "natural" attitude we are unable to ask the transcendental question: "How can we go beyond the island of consciousness?" Since we treat ourselves as already being "in the world" we cannot put ourselves in the questioning position, and thus we prejudge the problem of existence. But a similar argument may be applied to Husserl: Once I perform the "suspension" of existence on his terms, I prejudge the problem as well, and I cannot ask the transcendental question "how can I leave the island?" since it is already known that I will never leave it. Here the discussion must stop. Once we consent to put the question of "the bridge," we are committed to idealism. If we reject the question, then the realist or the idealist solution is a choice that depends on philosophical biases. The history of philosophy seems to teach, however, that all arguments in favor of either solution presuppose what is to be proved.

*How can other people exist?* If the subject who wants to discover the eidetic necessity and to restore the meaning of the world is bound to remain within his own limits, if "transcendence" itself is a meaning constituted in the Ego, the problem of solipsism and of the reality of alter ego naturally arises. How can we remain faithful to the principles of reduction and imagine the alter ego as being only intended but not constituted in

the same way as all other objects? We have now
arrived at what is perhaps the most obscure side of
Husserl's philosophy. It is clear that he wants to
avoid solipsism without renouncing his theory of
constitution, and that he is aware of the difficul-
ties of such an enterprise. He believes not only
that solipsism can be overcome but that this can
be done only within transcendental idealism. The
certitude he believed to have discovered was
intended to be universally valid—valid for any
rational being and accessible to everybody.

Does not the result contradict the intention?
Even if certitude is gained in this sense, nothing
can be concluded about the effective existence of
other rational beings, as long as we lack instruments giving us real contact with others, as long as
we lack a transcendental theory of empathy.
Husserl believes that the alter ego is constituted in
the intentional movement. The alter ego goes
beyond my monad; I constitute it as reflected in
my own ego. How is this possible? Husserl tries to
solve the question with the help of the second
epoché. Within the transcendental experience I
separate what is particularly *mine* from phenomena which are related to other egos as
subjects, for example cultural predicates that
imply a community of many subjects. What
remains after this exclusion is "Nature" (as the
meaning "Nature") including my own body and

my empirical ego as an object. And so it appears
that I, human ego, am constituted as a part of the
world and at the same time I am constituting all
objects, which is, he says, a paradox.

As transcendental ego, I separate what belongs
to me from the absolute, all-embracing, doubly
reduced ego, and within it I separate the realm of
its "owness" from the "otherness." I presuppose
that not all modes of my consciousness are modes
of my self-consciousness, that ego has an intentionality with the existence-sense, and with the
help of this intentionality it can go beyond its own
existence.

In constituting the world, I give it the sense of
being accessible to others' consciousness and
therefore (an unexpected conclusion) the first
non-ego I deal with is the alter ego, another
subject. This is the community of monads which
makes objective Nature possible. This transcendental intersubjectivity has its correlate in the
common world of experience.

The alter ego is "given" in my experience
personally, though not originally (which means,
apparently, simply that I do not participate
directly in his experience). My empathic sense of
him (or appresentation) is therefore indirect. This
does not mean that it consists in an intellectual
activity, or that it is an inference by analogy (from
behavior to subjectivity). It is an intuition of the

presence of another person as a subject. To me, my body has always the modus "here," and in empathy the other body in modus "there" indicates the same body in modus "here," i.e. the body is experienced by another monad as its own. Thus I see the body of another person as such, not as a symptom of another person. Still, the other person has the status of alter ego only as it is constituted within my transcendental field. The transcendental intersubjectivity of separated monads is formed *in me,* but as a community that is constituted in every other monad as well. My ego can know the world only in community with other egos, and only one monadologic community is possible (there cannot be many mutually opaque sets of monads, because when I think about them, they are not entirely opaque any more, I constitute them as a community). Consequently only one world and only one time are possible, and this world is bound to exist. And so, as Husserl points out at the end of his *Meditations,* the transcendental monadology yields some metaphysical results. Still, in no stage of this reflection do I abandon the epoché. I only explain the necessity of alter ego as a constituted meaning, and so I overcome solipsism while rejecting the naïve metaphysics of things in themselves. Transcendental intersubjectivity, being the absolute foundation, carries the world—and absolutely founded knowledge is based on universal self-knowledge.

In this crucial question of intersubjectivity, the unreliability of Husserl's universal method of achieving absolute certitude becomes especially glaring. His explanation is just as clumsy, even as it is obvious that he did everything possible within his construction to avoid solipsistic conclusions. After all his explanations, we still do not know how we reach another person as a real subjectivity. That we do not participate in others' experience is true but trivial. It is arguable that there is something like empathy—that I perceive another person as person and not as an automaton, not by inference or by analogy, and so on, but in a kind of special communication, different from other perceptions and not necessarily based on verbal contact (we may guess that a three-month-old baby communicates with adults, that there is a rudimentary understanding despite the lack of verbal contact, and certainly not by analogical inference). Many of Scheler's descriptions of this point are convincing. But to say this or to call this perception "appresentation" does not solve the problem of solipsism and does not need or imply the transcendental reduction. And the attempt to reconcile reduction with transcendental monadology cannot be performed without inconsistencies and without obscure speculative constructions. In the same fragment of *Meditations* Husserl says that alter ego precedes the common world of monads and that it is given in an indirect insight, by the intermediary of the body (which is a part of the world); that alter ego is the first non-ego; and that it is given as a result of the separation of those predicates that reveal the human community (hence, it is not first). I do not see how these statements are not contradictory.

My very ability to reach the alter ego is granted by a highly artificial and unconvincing construction: I carry out a second reduction which, within the transcendental ego, separates the ego proper and the "otherness." But it is unintelligible how within the transcendental field, which is present only as correlate of my transcendental acts, other egos could be constituted as being absolute *in the same sense* as I am. When I realize that only consciousness can be conceived as a self-supporting reality, this can only be *my* consciousness, or rather myself, a subject who imagines that he suspends belief in his own existence as a psychological subject. From this point of view other subjects cannot appear in the same form of independence. Alter ego cannot be anything else but a concretion of my consciousness. To say that I constitute all objects, and among them myself as an object, *is* self-contradictory; and to call a contradiction a paradox does not make it go away.

Husserl's monadology is for me another example of the logical hopelessness of all philosophical endeavors which start from subjectivity and try to restore the path toward the common world. It is so more significant that Husserl starts with transcendental, not psychological, subjectivity. His way of arguing for the reduction is first methodical: let us suspend belief in the reality of the world, including ego, since we find no certitude in it; let us concentrate on the contents of purified consciousness. However, once we stand on the ground of transcendental consciousness, we notice that it always has to do with a world that is made conscious. That the world is the "world-meaning," constituted in the consciousness; that the concept of things in themselves is absurd; that only consciousness is a self-supporting reality—all these are in Husserl variants of the traditional arguments of idealism. One cannot think about the world that is not being thought; once we think about the thing in itself, it becomes an object of thought, and thus the *concept* of the thing-in-itself, of a thing that is not an object of thought, ·is self-contradictory. This argument is irrefutable because tautological. Therefore Husserl's philosophy bears out Gilson's critique (addressed to Cartesians, Kantians, and those Christian realists who imitate Descartes and Kant): if we start with the immanent world, we will end in the immanent world, once we accept the idealist's way of asking, we accept his answer. Idealism cannot be overcome on the basis of its own question, on the basis of Cogito (I know directly only my own cogitationes, how to build a bridge from impressions or thoughts to the things). The problem of the bridge is insoluble; there is no logical passage. Therefore, according to Gilson, realism cannot be a conclusion from Cogito, only a method of thinking.

To say this does not mean to solve the question of "bridge," but to reject it. A question may be rejected either if it implies false presuppositions or if it is itself unintelligible. I will not engage in this eternal debate. What is wrong with all questions about the relation of "subjectivity" to the world is that we are not able to express them or to answer them except with the help of spatial symbols, while we know that what matters are not topological relations. Expressions like "*in* the consciousness," "within perception," "outside," "inside," "to be part of," "to reach the interior," "to stand before," "to be given directly," "immanent," "transcendent"—even the words "object," "subject," and "perception"—are all derivatives of spatial relationships and movements. Our descriptions seem to hinge necessarily on this spatial language, and they cannot get at the literal form.

Perhaps, as Bergson (who put up a special and not very successful effort to combat spatial analogies in describing consciousness) would have it, this is the lasting feature of language itself.

*The moral of the story*   Husserl's evolution from the ideal of unquestionable validity of knowledge to transcendental idealism suggests three remarks:

First, Husserl believed to have opened the way toward certitude in the sense of knowledge that is entirely independent of our status as biologically, culturally, and historically determined beings. To gain such an independence amounts to gaining the position of Gods, who can observe human (empirical) minds completely from the outside. At the same time he demanded that we should go back to the total freshness of mind, to a *tabula rasa* position, where our view of the world is not blurred in any way by language or by our cultural inheritance. He wanted philosophy to be in unmediated contact with things themselves and at the same time to be a rigorous science—to be communicable knowledge. These two tasks run counter to each other. A Catholic critic of Husserl, Quentin Lauer, remarked that Husserl, in trying to improve the Cartesian attempt, had failed to grasp the importance of the hypothetical demon in Descartes' reasoning. Since we cannot exclude the possibility of a diabolic will which

might pervert all our cognitive efforts and endow
the most fantastic delusions with the weight of
self-evidence, we realize that nothing is obvious
and nothing certain unless we believe in the
beneficent will of God, which prevents the devil
from leading us systematically into error. This is
true in the sense that the epistemological absolute
is indeed impossible without the ontological absolute, which combines the quality of being a
self-supporting ground of the world with perfect
wisdom and perfect goodness. Descartes was
wrong in believing that he had proved the
existence of the divine Creator, but he was
probably right in stating that this was only thanks
to divine omniscience and to trust in His veracity
that the foundation of certitude could be discovered.

Second, it is plausible to suspect, on the basis of
the development of the European philosophy from
Descartes onward, that if we start with Cogito, we
can reconstruct the world only as somehow correlated with subjectivity, unless we use some logically spurious devices like Descartes' divine veracity or Leibniz' pre-established harmony (this
theory giving us the guarantee that the perceptions of many monads, despite the lack of causal
relations between them, converge—which again
implies the divine mind). The converse relation is
probably valid, too. If we start with the thing or

"the being" in the sense of Parmenides or Spinoza, the categories applicable to it do not enable us to describe the irreducible subjectivity, this "miracle of miracles" (Husserl), this being-directed-toward-oneself, this act of experiencing oneself—unless we arbitrarily constitute it next to the world (as Spinoza did). It is very doubtful if anybody has succeeded in producing a language jointly encompassing these two viewpoints: one directed toward Cogito and the other directed toward things. It is possible that philosophy is fatefully condemned to oscillate between these two perspectives, each being arbitrary and each, once admitted, closing the way to the other, and both inexpressible together in the same discourse.

Finally, it is arguable—again, a moral from Husserl's development—that a truly radical search for certitude always ends with the conclusion that certitude is accessible only in immanence, that the perfect transparence of the object is to be found only when the object and subject (empirical or transcendental Ego, no matter) come to identity. This means that a certitude mediated in words is no longer certitude. We gain or we imagine to have gained access to certitude only as far as we gain or imagine to have gained perfect identity with the object, an identity whose model is the mystical experience. This experience however is incommunicable; any attempt to hand

it over to others destroys the very immediacy that
was supposed to be its value—consequently it
destroys certitude. Whatever enters the field of
human communication is inevitably uncertain,
always questionable, fragile, provisory, and mor-
tal. Still, the search for certitude is unlikely to be
given up, and we may doubt if it would be
desirable to stop it. This search has little to do
with the progress of science and technology. Its
background is religious rather than intellectual; it
is, as Husserl perfectly knew, a search for meaning. It is a desire to live in a world out of which
contingency is banned, where sense (and this
means purpose) is given to everything. Science is
incapable of providing us with that kind of
certitude, and it is unlikely that people could ever
give up their attempts to go beyond scientific
rationality.

I should end by saying that my intention was
not to suggest that Husserl's quest for the new
transcendental rationality and of the source of
perfect certainty was worthless. I think that his
attempt failed to reach its goal as indeed, I
suspect, all attempts to get at the epistemological
absolute are bound to fail. But I still consider his
work to be of tremendous value for our culture,
and this for two reasons. He better than anybody,

compelled us to realize the painful dilemma of knowledge: either consistent empiricism, with its relativistic, skeptical results (a standpoint which many regard discouraging, inadmissible, and in fact ruinous for culture) *or* transcendentalist dogmatism, which cannot really justify itself and remains in the end an arbitrary decision. I have to admit that although ultimate certitude is a goal that cannot be attained within the rationalist framework, our culture would be poor and miserable without people who keep trying to reach this goal, and it hardly could survive when left entirely in the hands of the skeptics. I do believe that human culture cannot ever reach a perfect synthesis of its diversified and incompatible components. Its very richness is supported by this very incompatibility of its ingredients. And it is the conflict of values, rather than their harmony, that keeps our culture alive.